Bread & Dripping Days

Kathleen McArthur
Bread & Dripping Days
An Australian Growing Up in the 20's

Kangaroo Press

Illustrated by David Bromley

©Kathleen McArthur 1981

First published in 1981
Reprinted in 1982
by Kangaroo Press
3 Whitehall Road, Kenthurst 2154
Typeset by GT Setters Pty Ltd
Printed in Hong Kong by Bookbuilders Ltd

ISBN 0 949924 11 3

Contents

Favourite Foods	7
Sunday roast	8
Bread and dripping	9
Shepherd's pie	10
Pie-melons	11
Regular Routine	12
Cleaning	12
Saturday morning	13
Maiden aunt	15
Hair	16
Sunday and Monday	18
Thursday	19
Sunday drive	20
Annual Events	22
Anzac Day	22
St Patrick's Day	24
Blanket wash	24
Punishment	25
The Exhibition	25
The Company picnic	26
School	28
Hawaiian culture	30
Australian ballads	31
Recitations	32
School readers	32
Basketball	34
Teasing	36
Stories	38
Summer Holidays	41
Irish cousins	41
The tradespeople	44
Climbing trees	45
Lobbies	47

The Old House	49
Vegetable garden	52
Mrs Wall	52
Haunted House	53
Green frogs	54
Daisy chains	54
Underneath the house	55
Possums, flying foxes and dingoes	55
Brothers and Sisters	56
Little boys	56
Opera	57
At the Dinner Table	61
The End of an Era	63

Favourite Foods

When butter was sixpence a pound children ate dry bread, or bread and dripping.

                Mary Gilmour in *Old Days Old Ways*

Since World War Two Australians have been imbued with culinary culture. They have been taught to put away their old bad ways of eating, to learn from the French, the Indonesians, the Indians, the Spanish, the Chinese, to bring fresh flavours into food, to use lots of herbs, fresh herbs of course, to use vegetable oils in place of animal fats, to be innovative, to be daring, to open up the horizons of their eating habits, to learn what wines to drink with certain foods and to abhor that habit of calling the family to the dinner table when the teapot is brought in, kept warm in its gaily coloured woollen jumper. Everything we did in the past was wrong. Why, we even called a stew a stew and into it went anything lying around the kitchen or the kitchen garden or the ice-chest. A stew is no longer a stew unless it is an Irish stew; now it is goulash or pot-au-feu or ragout or boeuf bourguignon and they come from large, glossy cookbooks full of fine colour photography. Country Women and Presbyterian Ladies now move into history with Mrs Beeton. We used to be so ignorant and we have been made to feel ashamed of the old days and old ways, in adopting the new.

Sunday roast

So, we no longer worship before the Sunday roast; that succulent roll of beef or leg of mutton or the crackling-topped joint of pork with the roast potatoes and onions and pumpkin and the boat of gravy to pour all over it. That was not the end of the meal, of course, it could have been followed by steamed golden-syrup pudding with rich egg custard. It is just not on now. Our smart friends would despise us for our backwardness, would probably point us out to their friends like they would do to someone who hasn't yet got colour TV, as the poor, the ignorant, the deprived. Smart members of today's elite society have a porta-gas barbecue for cooking their rump steaks, which are washed down with a vintage year Hunter Valley claret. They know the ropes! They are executive material who have to hold their own with their competitive fellows who invite them to Sunday luncheon of chicken legs and champagne, around the pool. And what is just as essential, is to be dressed in the right gear, whether the right gear is the latest in high fashion or op-shop fun clothes. Sunday roasts and Sunday best clothes might have been good enough for our parents—those dear, funny old people who hadn't the advantages of the culture brought to this country by our post-war migrants. It needs to be remembered that we are speaking of the days when only Jesus Christ had long hair and a beard and wore a kaftan.

Just thinking about that roast dinner makes one nostalgic, secretly of course. We remember how it was when we were young and we begin to recall how we used to live in those far off backward years before the war, when the air was clean and sex was dirty and houses were built of wood and their roofs were iron and the rain rained harder then; rain on a hot tin roof is never to be forgotten. And, oh for shame, there might have been a dunny in the backyard and probably a chook-run too, into which were thrown the kitchen scraps.

Bread and dripping

If we are going to be nostalgic in thinking about the Sunday roast, whatever happened to bread and dripping? Tell the young, with drooling mouth, about bread and dripping and they open their eyes wide and

say, 'What's dripping?' After the long walk home from school there was bread and dripping for afternoon tea, liberally sprinkled with pepper and salt. In sheep districts it was mutton dripping and those children swore it was the best, but the cattle families plumbed for beef dripping as the tastiest. Nothing was ever heard of pork dripping, probably because pig-breeders grew so fond of their charges they couldn't bear to kill their darlings for their own consumption. It would be like eating one's own friends—straight out cannabalism. While you may slaughter a bullock, kill a sheep—this little pig goes to market.

> This little pig went to market,
> This little pig stayed home,
> This little pig had roast beef,
> This little pig had none,
> And this little pig cried, Wee, wee, wee!
> I can't find my way home.

Shepherd's pie

There was a sequel to the Sunday roast which was Monday's shepherd's pie. Children were allowed to—no, correction, would most willingly assemble the mincer, that old, black cast-iron, manual mincer that nowadays would most likely only be found in a folk museum. It was screwed on to the end of the scrubbed-down, deal, kitchen table with a pad of folded paper beneath the grabs, so they would not leave unsightly impressions in the soft wood.

Into the mouth of the mincer would go the chunks of meat, alternately with onion, carrot and herbs from the garden, sage and marjoram (some people used fresh herbs even then), but definitely no garlic for those were pre-garlic days, at least for respectable families. A bread crust or two might stretch out the volume if need be but that would be put through last to soak up whatever juices might be in the bowl of the mincer. Most of the liquid was caught in a basin below. A few bits and pieces escaped from the mouth of the mincer into the mouth of the mincer behind the mincer. That was a mincer's right! Some Worcester sauce and possibly tomato sauce as well was mixed in and, of course if any gravy was left from yesterday's dinner that was added too, and the mixture was placed in an enamel baking dish and topped with a thick crust of mashed potato, on the surface of which a pattern was executed with a fork, in relief, which came out of the oven beautifully tinted brown and gold—a work of art even if it was only folk art.

Sometime during the preparation Mother would remark: 'Shepherd's pie, Captain Johnson must be in port.' Captain Johnson was the captain of a Howard Smith coastal tramp steamer. He was popular with the children and was mercilessly teased by the head of the house who was always saying, 'Harry knows every sand-bank on the Australian coast. He's been on them all.' Harry got his own back on his host who had been a ship's engineer. It was probably the traditional banter between the bridge and the engine room for it certainly was always friendly.

Pie-melons

Still on the food of our cultural past—where have all the pie-melons gone? They used to be everywhere, just for the picking-up and they went into deep-crusted pies with ginger or pineapple, or lemon, or dried apricots—what was left over from the huge batches of jam, that is. Remember the cutting-up? Great team work, that was. Everyone sat around the kitchen table, cutting the pale-green flesh into cubes, removing the millions of seeds, and dumping it all into the preserving pan in the centre. Was it really fun, as it seems to be at this distance in time, or was it the drudgery of women's past, as we are now being told it was? Have pie-melons actually died out from sheer neglect, or have they, like gravy been driven underground to be indulged in, in secret? And yet, when one begins to recall the past as it was, surely pie-melons grew from the summer picknicker's water-melon seed, left to grow undisturbed, until the next holiday period, probably at Easter.

Being fussy about food was not permitted. Every child had to eat 'what was good for you', even parsnips and Swede turnips if fathers liked them. They were 'kronk' in the children's vernacular of the day. 'When I grow up I'll never eat cabbage,' to which a mother would reply, 'I said just that when I was your age and it is funny that when I grew up I liked cabbage.' She might have been right about cabbage but not about parsnips and Swede turnips.

Regular Routine

Cleaning

Cleanliness was most respectable. It seemed to be compulsory as though one's standing in the community depended upon it. Maybe it did but cleanliness was rather taken to extremes when verandahs were scrubbed. The old Queensland houses often had white beech verandah floors which could be kept beautifully white with scrubbing, but, of course, at the same

time showed up every spot of dirt or stain. What was popular with the children and more fun for all than scrubbing was hosing-down, when the child held the hose and an adult swished the water around with a millet broom. There was still another method used and that was to save the tea-leaves and sweep the verandah with those. This at least kept the dust down. But there were aspects of long-ago living that are best forgotten, like cleaning the knives and cleaning the silver, that fancy Victorian silver that had squiggly patterns that made the job so difficult, it had to be done with an old toothbrush. That was undeniably a drudgery, but at least it didn't happen every day, after every meal as did knife-cleaning before the days of stainless steel. Was it sand-soap, or Bon Ami or Monkey Brand that was used for cleaning knives? The subject is not entertaining so we will switch to another aspect of our cultural, almost colonial past—the bush house where mothers found relaxation with their potting; recycling holed saucepans, broken-spouted tea-pots, handle-less jugs, maybe even a chamber pot; anything that could hold some soil and grow a plant.

Saturday morning

After fifty years, sisters will get together and say: 'Do you remember those Saturday mornings?' The routine was so strict, it was almost a ritual, but it ended on a light note when it was permitted to slippery slide into the bath. Let us take Saturday morning step by step. Before breakfast there was the cup of senna-tea which was somehow acceptable when mother made it, but ghastly and revolting when the maiden aunt gave it out when she was in charge. It was a well-known and acceptable fact amongst children that maiden aunts did not know how to do things the right way; and they were ugly too, not beautiful like mothers. You might sometimes be sorry for them but much more sorry for yourself when they were in charge. Blow, blow, thou winter wind, thou art not so unkind as ungrateful children.

Senna-tea, then breakfast and the washing-up done and the beds stripped and made up with fresh sheets, not forgetting the top to bottom dodge. Just to think of it brings back the smell of unbleached calico. The smell that acted like a drug to lull the young into a sense of security and peaceful sleep. Beds made, finger nails and toe nails cut and then came the preparation

for the hair washing, with its little secret. Hair was massaged with olive-oil and into that oil had been put two drops of kerosene and that was to ensure that the children of nice, clean, God-fearing (and lice fearing) Christian parents escaped the stigma of that whispered terrible word 'nits'.

Preparation complete, the Saturday bath began. It was different from the baths of the other days of the week because of two things, the hair-washing and the play that was allowed before the final dipper of cold water over the head, then out and dried. The bath game was an awful wet mess but it was tremendous fun. The rim of the bath was well soaped (they were not walled in then), and the little bottoms swung around the curved end and slipped down the back, splash into the water, sending an enormous tidal wave over the sides and on to the bathroom floor. Did our Mother mind? If she did there is no recollection of any reprimand. They are such beautiful people, mothers are—or were.

Maiden aunt

Nostalgia is terribly infectious so long as the memories are all pleasant. Because of that guilty feeling we suffer when we remember the way we treated the maiden aunt, we want to make up for it by recalling something nice about her, and of course there were lots of nice things about her. She would give us sixpence, which was a great bonus, for brushing her long hair, and she had time to sit at the piano and play old favourites of her generation, which the kids joined in, singing with more noise than sentiment. 'Right, children, after you've done the washing-up we will have a singsong.' It was straight out bribery; the use of child labour at its worst, but we were not then up to the Industrial Revolution at school. Remember 'The Bells of St Mary's', 'Roses of Picardy', 'Bonnie Annie Laurie', 'My Little Grey Home in The West'? The sessions were never complete without 'Danny Boy'— Londonderry Air, mother's favourite.

With sisters on nostalgia trips, discussing those days, there is a question that comes up frequently, 'I wonder what happened to *that*'. There was that exquisite little model of the Taj Mahal, remember it? Maiden Aunt had been an Army Nursing Sister towards the end of the First War and for several years afterwards and had brought home from India that model among other fascinating exotic souvenirs. We can only suppose she gave it to a nephew or niece who was nicer to her than we were. Children seem much nicer when they are not seen quite as often as we were.

Hair

It must have been before the days of short hair and the permanent wave, when ladies still had long hair and competed over its length. It was not worth boasting about the length unless it was at least long enough to sit on. Otherwise, someone would know someone who had hair down to her knees. Imagine the hairpins needed to pin that up! If the hair was straight, the little curls around the face had to be made with hot tongs. Some mothers could not compete in the long hair stakes and had to cheat by wearing a 'bun'. It probably had a more stylish name but it was a bun to the children. It was false pretences indeed, pretending to own a 'fine head of hair' when there was not enough at the back to fill a thimble. What was needed to create this bun was a thing like a fly swish without a handle and made from someone else's hair of the same colour. It was rolled up and pinned with numerous hairpins at the back of the head and, when a hat was worn, the hairpins went right through the middle of it.

It may have been because Mother lacked a crowning glory and her first three girls inherited that fine, wispy top of hers that she was so proud of little sister's plaits. Dad thought they were great too, having precious little left of his own corn silk. The whole family admired little sister's hair from which the poor child suffered dreadfully, not from having it brushed and plaited every day (which surprisingly she enjoyed) but from having the knots combed out after the Saturday hair treatment. It hurt her and she cried and that hurt everyone else because we loved her dearly and it was distressing to hear her cry. But NO! She could *not* have it cut! How terribly cruel everyone was! It was not until her twelfth birthday on the eve of going away to boarding school, that the reprieve came. No one would do it at home, she had to be taken to a barber (or was it a hairdresser?) for them to be cut off 'entire', for Mother to tie them with ribbon and put away with her treasures. And that, little sister recalls, left her with a most peculiar hair style.

Despite the weekly hair treatment, the curse sometimes fell on the innocent children through the school week. Just a thoughtless little scratch of the head and the fine comb would be brought out and the hair combed with it over a pillow. It was nearly as much fun as watching the monkeys at the zoo.

There was a girl, we can call her Belle because that wasn't her name; she had big brown freckles on white skin and auburn ringlets, a most distinctive looking child. Whoever sat in the desk behind her was treated to a most unusual entertainment that completely distracted attention from the lesson. Down a ringlet would crawl a louse, round and round it descended, following the strand of hair until it got to the bottom where it would pause while it made up its mind where to go from there. Would it drop off? No, apparently it did not think it would be safer elsewhere, and it was probably right, so back up the ringlet it crawled, round and round again until it finally disappeared. What was the teacher saying?

Bridesmaid

It must happen quite often when one sister is chosen to be a bridesmaid or a flower-girl at a wedding, or to play a very special role which is the envy of her sisters. That Bread and Dripping Days Mother knew exactly how to handle such a situation, so by handing on to today's mothers some of her wisdom, it may ease a similar difficult situation.

'Never mind, dear,' she promised, 'you can be my bridesmaid when I get married.'

And when the child tells everyone the good news she gets the sweetest smiles from them all, showing that they were pleased too.

Sunday and Monday

Sunday had its routine also when, after early church, mother soaked the soiled clothes in preparation for the Monday wash. Children were not very good at that, probably because their hearts were not in the chore but they could and were sometimes allowed to use the broken-off, rusty laundry knife to pare the soap for the copper, and measure out the washing soda and fill the copper with the hose. Everything possible had to be done on Sunday because the laundress—(no, not a laundress, she was 'the washerwoman') arrived on Monday morning while it was still dark. She had a rival down the road, whom in fact she did not know but they competed for being the first out with hanging the wash. Rival washerwomen communicated solely by mental telepathy or perhaps they could hang the tea towels in order to send a message, as flags are hung on ships and lighthouses. Those were gayer times, and freer was the washing when lines spread out so far they had to be propped up with trimmed saplings brought around the streets by a man with a horse and cart, calling his wares 'clothes props'. Of

course, as a trade it did not boost the economy in the manner of Hill's Hoists.

Monday afternoon, after school, children helped to fold the sheets and were allowed to iron the handkerchiefs. More child labour, but with such willing labourers.

The cleanliness next to godliness precept was not only for outside appearances, as internal cleanliness was also practised diligently and not unpleasantly except, repeat, (oh, it can stir up revulsion after fifty years at the very thought of it) except if one had to be given a dose of castor oil. Nothing in growing up was

worse. So we will forget about it and continue with the old-fashioned preventative medicine. Apart from the weekly cup of senna-tea, there was sulphur and treacle between seasons which was to keep the skin clear and healthy. Kepler's cod-liver oil and malt kept winter colds away and liquid magnesia cooled the blood in midsummer. Fruit last thing at night was considered bad, so it is no wonder there was so much tooth decay. The old adage that 'fruit is gold in the morning, silver at noon, and lead at night' had apparently slipped unnoticed into the twentieth century and was still going strong in the 1920s.

Thursday

Thursday was mending day. Why Thursday? Well, at this distance in time, the answer to that query has to be reasoned out. Saturday was children-cleaning day in the morning and children visiting day in the afternoon (never 'arvo' for that was unpermissible slang), when other children came to play. Sunday was family day, with church in the morning (Dad only went to church on Anzac Day). There was a compulsory after-dinner quiet to aid digestion of that big midday meal, then possibly a drive if there were no callers, but Sunday afternoon was a traditional calling time. Monday was washing day with damping-down in the afternoon in preparation for the ironing on Tuesday. So much was starched in those days, like tablecloths and serviettes, collars and cuffs of gentlemen's shirt for a beginning. Wednesday was cleaning day so, with Friday devoted to baking for the coming week, Thursday seems a logical choice.

So it was on Thursday that the clothes were mended; socks were darned, collars and cuffs were turned and sheets turned too, side to centre. Then there were the hand-me-downs the family had grown out of, which also had to be mended and buttons sewn on before being carefully folded and packed for sending to the 'creche', whatever that was. Sheets too far gone for repair were stripped and rolled into bandages which also went to the creche. The children took those neatly woven darns and neat patches for granted, only realizing their beauty a generation later.

Sunday drive

Before leaving the weekdays, let us take a Sunday drive, or just a small section of one. Dad often called at 'the office' which was in the city. From there we would be driven past the Botanic Gardens, but it was what was to be seen on the footath on the opposite side of the road from the Gardens that most interested and puzzled us. There would be a row of ladies sitting in chairs, wearing dressing gowns (in the afternoon, and smoking cigarettes). Surprisingly there was no conversation about it. Very puzzling indeed.

Annual Events

Weekly events were a matter of course, but there were also annual events, some pleasant and others not so pleasant. One most memorable one was a visit from a country cousin of the older generation, a bachelor who produced whole packets, not just single strips, but whole packets of chewing gum—taboo for the rest of the year, because the children of respectable, God-fearing, good Christian families did not chew gum.

Anzac Day

A less pleasant annual event was Anzac Day when the man of the house re-fought the war and boasted of his daring deeds with an unaccustomed wildness. It was rather frightening, seeing a normally kindly, fun-loving parent turned into such a fearsome creature. More unpleasant still were the tears the woman of the house, shed for a favourite brother who had been killed at Gallipoli. Not a good day and what was more, it was a holiday without a picnic. There is a very dim memory of an Anzac Day procession which was watched from the balcony of a Webster's Cafe in Queen Street, when that handsome father, looking more handsome still in his uniform, rode a spirited horse down the street below and waved his riding crop at us. It must have been not long after the war, probably 1919 or 1920, thus accounting for the fading picture.

St Patrick's Day

Another procession was watched from the same place later, as guests of our Irish cousins down from the western plains—the St Patrick's Day procession. The picture of that procession has completely faded away but not the stories told by our cousins about their Irish uncles. They told us that St Patrick's Day on the station began with the Irish uncles raising the Irish Flag and then, below it, the Union Jack. This was too much for the second generation born cousins who waited until the uncles were out of the way then pulled down the flags and reversed the precedence. From their hiding places they never failed to witness the expected fireworks when the uncles discovered the treason.

Blanket wash

Then there was the annual blanket wash when the children were allowed to jump up and down on the lather-filled blankets in the tubs. It was another example of unpaid child labour, when you come to think of it. On the other hand, it was probably the one day of the year when everyone had spotlessly clean feet.

At that time, we were blissfully unaware that there were children who did not have blankets but slept under cornsacks or sugar-bags stitched together and lined with newspaper, and anyway they may not have had tubs either, for their washing was done out of doors in four-gallon kerosene tins over open fires, provided of course there was enough water in the creek. One thing though we would have envied those children was going barefoot. Having to wear shoes had nothing to do with social status or respectability, it was solely a preventative against hookworm, which had not then been wiped out as it was later.

Some children in dairy-farm districts who had no shoes had a way of keeping their feet warm when walking to school on cold, frosty winter mornings by running from one fresh, warm cowpat to the next.

Punishment

Punishment for naughtiness was not severe. For bad table manners came the order 'take it on to the door mat', but it was never enforced, the insult worked alone. For cheeky speech, it was to be sent into a corner, facing inwards—an indignity that first induced anger, expressed under the breath, 'Mother is a pig. Mother is a pig.' But as time wore on and no relief came, repentance was the only alternative.

Now and then the commanding officer himself needed a little punishment, being late home for dinner, for instance. 'Let's punish him!'

'How?'

'We'll have a secret from him.'

'What'll it be?'

'I know', said Mother, 'I'll get another baby and we won't tell him anything about it.'

In the enthusiasm, the idea of punishment was forgotten. But who could have foreseen the consequences? The very next morning the local M.L.A., driving past in his sulky, picked up one of the children and dropped her off at the school; time enough to be informed that 'Mother is getting another baby and Daddy doesn't know anything about it.'

The Exhibition

It is not until you have done it yourself that you learn what an endurance test it is taking five children to the Exhibition. The children of nice, respectable, God-fearing, good Christian-living parents did not say 'The Ekka' then. That was slang and properly brought-up children did not use slang. Fifty years ago bags of samples were often free and even if they weren't free, they were cheap, and so, after going right through the Industrial Pavilion, everyone was laden down like packhorses and the wise parent then shepherded the children into the grandstand to watch the trotting or the high jump or the sheep-dog trials which the wise parent probably did watch, but the children had their little curly heads inside those numerous bags, putting Faulding's eau-de-cologne on their clothes, eating Webster's biscuits and Plumridges jelly beans and swopping a Commonwealth Bank ruler for a writing pad with a film star cover. Two most desirable products were wished for with renewed annual emotion but never ever obtained. They were the fluffy doll on the fine, black walking stick and the ride on the Ferris wheel. Mother knows best even if her children consider themselves deprived. Children are too precious to be killed or have their eyes poked out.

Mother always had to see the pigs. She loved pigs, did Mother, so the children went along to the pig pens, too, protesting about the smell. Mother said it

was a healthy smell but that made eldest sister protest even harder. Eldest sister insisted on refinement in all things and, true to character, she still does. One could safely bet she has not seen a pig since her childhood days. In fact she always has disliked anything rural, and why anyone should choose to live in the country is quite beyond her comprehension.

The Company picnic

The Company picnic was an eagerly looked-forward-to annual event. Preparation seemed to go on for a week beforehand, and such fascinating preparation some of it was, especially the brawn-making from half a pig's head. The children were goggle-eyed with interest while watching the meat extracted from between the bones and all put into a press, coming out from it eventually in a wonderful pattern of reddish, jellied meat. It was fascinating to look at, as were also beetroot set in aspic and patterned salads, but the best food at the Company picnic was what *other* people brought, like the griddle scones the Scottish mothers made. Some mothers, known to us, were hopelessly inefficient in not knowing how to make mealy griddle scones. It was probably because they were Australian; maybe mothers needed to be Scottish and say 'och' and 'aye' to be able to make griddle scones.

Even better remembered about those days of the Company picnic was the free ice cream and the Perkins ginger beer in casks, as much as you could eat and drink, provided by the Company. It was unfortunate but acceptable that, while you could enjoy the feasting, it was not possible to win the foot races afterwards, too.

School

While home was the most important thing in life because that was where there was security in the warmth of loving parents and the familiar things like one's own bed, school also meant a lot, for that was where your friends were. Such interesting friends they could be too. That girl with the beautiful teeth, without any fillings, who had never been to a dentist

and did not even own a toothbrush. Toothbrushes, we were lectured, were to save you the suffering at the dentist's. It rather undermined the child's faith in the wisdom of the parents to find that, while *you* had to 'clean your teeth and say your prayers' every morning before school and still went to the dentist, someone else, who did not even own a toothbrush, should have perfect teeth. That was probably where the questioning of authority actually began.

Then there was Rex, a person of distinction. We were proud to live in her reflected glory because she was a niece of Snowy Baker. What! You have never heard of Snowy Baker? Well, perhaps nobody now could be expected to know who Snowy Baker was, but at that time everyone knew his name because he was a great horseman in Australia and then became a star in silent movies: an Australian success in Hollywood. A child would need an uncle Prime Minister to beat that—or the Pope!

Another friend always had two shillings to spend when others had only pennies. She was everyone's friend until she was found out. And yet another friend was enviously well-dressed in her pink crepe with the flared skirt and a pair of Mary Pickford shoes in black patent leather. It was thought that she was as beautiful and as smart as Mary Pickford herself.

There were boyfriends too. Everyone in the class knew whose boyfriend was whose even though nothing ever passed between them but looks, looks full of what today are called 'vibes'. How about having the captain of the school cricket team for your boyfriend? The status of that was unrivalled.

There were also the hopeful but unsuccessful attempts at establishing friendships between little boys and little girls. Bars of chocolate were most desirable courting gifts for little girls, presented

discreetly through a young brother, but never, never could a little girl accept them, however tempting, from a boy who had elastic in the hem of his pants. The happy little brother go-between scored everytime. That same little girl remembered the unacceptable presents from the boy with elastic in the hem of his pants when, during the war, he, a surgeon commander then, was reported lost when his ship was torpedoed.

They were slate and slate pencil days; squeak, squeak, squeak, scratch, scratch, scratch was the classroom noise as the children wrote on their slates whilst another sense was abused: the sense of smell when the slate-rag tins were opened. Whew! They stank.

Old school slates still turn up in op-shops but slate pencils cannot be bought for love or money. A good substitute is the quill of a sea urchin. They scratch well on slates.

Next door to the school was a Church home for girls. The girls were what would be referred to today as the children of single parent families. They were nice girls and popular but there was nevertheless a felt rather than expressed stigma attached to the 'home' girls. Two of them always sang a duet in the school concerts and the song they usually sang was 'Two Little Girls in Blue', but the significance of the words, while the singers themselves would have been aware of it, was lost on the young audience who knew no less than two parents. As it is remembered, these were the words:

> Two little girls in blue, lad,
> Two little girls in blue;
> They were sisters, we were brothers
> Who learnt to love them true.
> One little girl in blue, lad,
> Who won your father's heart,
> Became your mother.
> I married the other,
> But we have drifted apart.

Hawaiian culture

Hawaiian culture was in vogue in those days. (Was the word 'culture' even in the popular vocabulary then?) There was never a school fancy-dress ball without the usual girls in their home-made, natural-coloured raffia skirts, crepe-paper leis and anklets, frangipanni flowers in the hair. So it is not surprising to remember that an item in a school concert in that funny little Shire Hall (redeemed by having a stage, which was more than the school possessed) was a chorus of young Hawaiians, seated cross-legged on the floor of the stage, swaying the torso left and right and making rhythmic arm movements, three beats to the left, three beats to the right to this Hawaiian song:

King Ke-me-ha-me-ha, (*switch arms over to the right*)
  The con-queror of the is-lands, (*left again*)
  Be-came a fam-ous her-o one day. (*right again*)
  He fought a nat-ive ar-my (*left*)
  And pushed it o'er the pali (*right*)
  And crowned himself King of Hawaii.

Were the Polynesian language lines in the song omitted as too difficult—for the children to sing or the teachers to teach?

It is strange under what circumstances some things are recalled. That little memory would possibly have been lost forever if it had not been for a tour of the Hawaiian Islands two of the sisters made more than fifty years later, during which they were taken to a little place called Kohala, the birthplace of that Hawaiian king on the Big Island which is what they call the island of Hawaii, to see a magnificent bronze statue of Kemehameha in feather cloak and all. Gradually it all returned and yet there were some doubts about the authenticity of the memory, but these were all dispelled when a music shop produced the song on a little 45 record.

It was on that same island, as we walked across the crater of the still alive volcano of Kilauea, we remembered the fiery picture Dad had of the same spot as a souvenir of his days in the Pacific cable service. Sadly, the time had passed when we could talk to him about it.

Australian ballads

Town people had not begun to sing Australian ballads then, songs like 'Click Go The Shears' or even 'Waltzing Matilda'. Australian songs were still restricted to the campfire, the shearing sheds, the railway fettlers' camps and cane-cutters barracks. Many of the words were known from the publications of Banjo Patterson, but they were presented as recitations, not songs. Another thirty years had to wait for the music of our folklore to be collected and first offered to the public, but it certainly soon made up for lost time in becoming popular.

Recitations

'Will you recite that new poem for the ladies?' Mother is having an afternoon tea-party. The ladies are sitting straight-backed in their well-corseted outfits; hats, gloves and all. We have done the rounds and presented our cheeks whenever asked 'Aren't you going to give me a kiss?' The atmosphere is cold to the senses of the children as though both hostess and guests were fulfilling an obligation. The child's obligation is to recite her piece and escape as soon as politeness permits.

The Little Plant

In the heart of a seed
Buried deep, so deep,
A dear little plant
Lay fast asleep.

'Wake!' said the sunshine
'And creep to the light.'
'Wake!' said the voice
Of the raindrops bright.

The little plant heard,
And it rose to see
What the wonderful
Outside world might be.

Kate L. Brown

School readers

Do your sisters remember that first red school reader? No, they don't. Every story with a moral, just as the preface said: 'Many of the readings convey simple moral lessons in a form suitable for children.' There was 'The Ass in The Lion's Skin', the moral of which was, 'Those who pretend to be what they are not are laughed at when they are found out.' The moral of the two buckets in the well was 'There are two ways of looking at things. If you wish to be happy, look on the bright side.'

> The little boy who says 'I'll try',
> Will climb to the hill-top;
> The little boy who says 'I can't',
> Will at the bottom stop.

Moralists are still trying to influence children with that one, as we know from *Jonathan Livingstone Seagull*, and the adults are still lapping it up.

Just in case the child was not bright enough to see the point of the story by himself, it was carefully spelt out at the end of each story: 'We should never boast of what we know, or of what we can do. Those who can do most boast least.'

It was probably a school reader of this kind that had goaded Norman Lindsay into creating his *Magic Pudding* with its delightfully irreverent characters.

Does anyone remember the frontispiece in the reader? It is a picture of a class, standing toes to line, in a school shed, each with a book in hand before a female teacher seated on a chair. The caption below is 'The New Reading Books (see Lesson 22)'. Lesson 22 is titled 'Books' and it begins with these words: 'Look at the first picture in this book. How happy the children seem.' Nonsense! It is outrageous brainwashing. They neither look happy nor unhappy. They do look well-disciplined and well-dressed, with every child in shoes and socks. Perhaps only the best-dressed were selected for such an important picture, going into the front of the book; which would have been in keeping with the hypocrisy throughout. It should here seem obvious that some children did not learn the important lesson of always looking at the bright side of things.

Strange are the associations of thoughts. Mother had a very small ricepaper recipe book that looked rather like an expensive prayerbook, so the children were allowed to take it to church. Looking devout, at the same time they could learn how to cut up an ox. One never knew when such information might come in handy. Hadn't Mother said to one of us: 'With your appetite you had better marry a butcher when you grow up'?

Basketball

Dad had a theory—he was a great producer of theories, like no fruit at bedtime. This other one must have come straight out of the mid-nineteenth century, which was that we all should wear woollen singlets winter *and* summer. Oh, the memory of playing basketball in summer wearing a woollen singlet will survive at least those three score years and ten. Dad did not give up the habit himself for many years but we children, at great risk to our health, he let it be known, were allowed to be excused, on protest.

Getting into the basketball team at ten years of age was a great ambition achieved. It meant that every Friday of the season there was a grand adventure in going with the team and a teacher by tram or train or both, to visit schools all over Brisbane—even as far as Myrtletown. Nothing seems to happen in Myrtletown that would get it into the news; it had simply ceased to exist for over fifty years, so it was really exciting to find it is still there, rediscovered in the Postcode Book, 4008. It took the team half a day to get to Myrtletown, first by tram into the city and

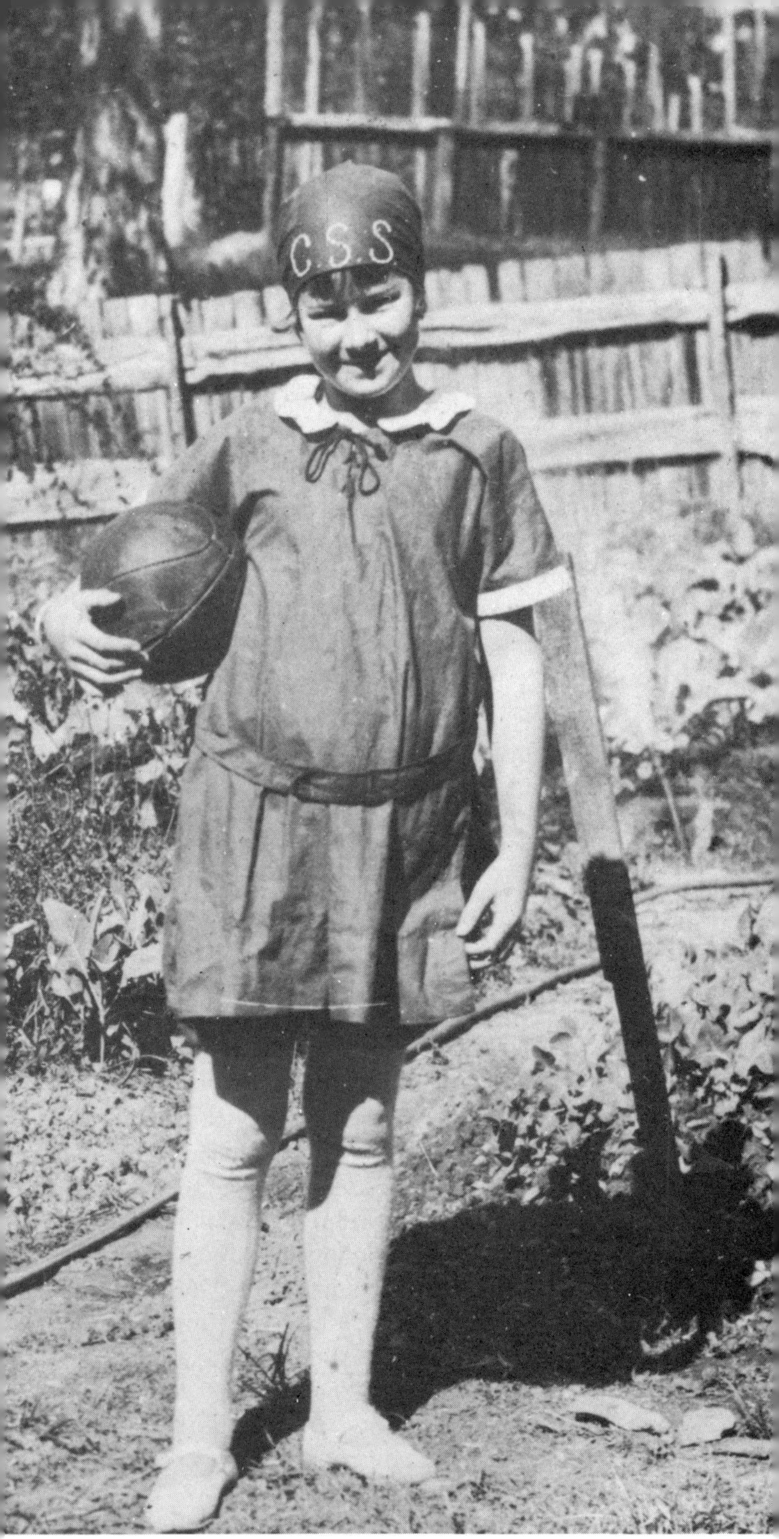
C.S.S

then by train right down the north shore of the Brisbane River to somewhere near Pinkenba. Memory insists that the train actually stopped at a place clearly marked 'Myrtletown'. The school there was very small and we beat them easily.

One school which beat us hollow was the Central Practising School right in the centre of the city. (There must have been a reason for a school being given such an extraordinary name.) The basketball field there was sealed with bitumen and surrounded by a high wire fence which was unusual. It was quite a hilarious game because the CPS girls were older and the ten-year-old found herself defending against a tall thirteen-year-old who was at least a metre taller, so she hardly touched the ball right through the game. Those two girls, the tall and the short of them, still laugh about that game, for they have been friends ever since.

Teasing

Being the Ugly Duckling of the family is no problem when there is plenty of warm affection all about. As Mother used to say and she had a saying for every occasion:

> My face I don't mind it
> for I am behind it.
> It's those in the front get the jar.

But to have to live with the prophecy of growing-up 'to be short and fat like Grandma' (there was only one) was an intolerable threat.

Hadn't some one said that we grow while we are asleep? You would wonder how they found that out, wouldn't you? There was nothing else for it but to put it to the test. Every night before settling down to sleep, the body was stretched out as long as it would go, while at the same time the retroussé nose had to be pulled straight to put an end to that bit of tiresome teasing. It worked. So 'they' were right, the Ugly Duckling grew to an acceptable five foot four inches, not equal to her tall elegant mother and sisters, but it was at least a good deal taller than short, fat Grandma. And she wears a straight nose to this day.

Some children will take a lot of teasing, secure in the knowledge of being loved: 'Where did I come from?' asked one sister of her mother. 'You came out of a beautiful white rose.' 'And where did I come from,' asked the Ugly Duckling. 'You! You came out of a grubby cabbage.' But it can make them grow up with an entirely false picture of themselves.

Bread and Dripping Days were giggling days. There are no more requirements to set up a giggle session than for someone to begin, because it is highly infectious among little girls. On the other hand, certain words, dirty words, of course, could spark one off. How about this for starters?

There was a little fly and he flew into a store
and he pooped on the ceiling and he pooped on the floor
and he pooped on the lollies and he pooped on the jam
and he pooped all over the grocery man.

The grocery man he got his little gun
to shoot that little fly on his little brown bum,
but before he could count five or ten
the little brown fly poop pooped agen.

A little bit of miming made it even naughtier.

Stories

In childhood we were not great readers; there was always something to do and someone to play with. And while there were plenty of books about they held little interest. The stories were so unreal, it was impossible to believe in them, or they were so terribly sad you couldn't see the print through the tears. May Gibbs and Ida Rentoul Outhwaite did not stir our Australian feelings, and anyway we were partial to Banksia Men, and Beatrix Potter couldn't compete with real possums, flying foxes, howling dingoes, or mother in the garden killing snakes with the hoe. Norman Lindsay's *Magic Pudding* would have been just right but it only came into our lives when we thought we were too old for it, whereas in fact we were not yet old enough to appreciate it fully. It might be assumed that Norman Lindsay's reputation prejudged any children's book he might write to be 'quite unsuitable' without having any knowledge of its contents.

On the other hand we loved Dad's and Mother's stories, particularly Mother's stories about life on the cattle station in the Kimberleys where she had lived with her brother and their cousins for some years before marrying Dad. Because she was in those stories, they were real and there was living drama in them, with cousins being speared by blacks, and stockmen drowning in flooded creeks; stories about the amusing household gins whom she obviously loved and who had given her a 'husband beater' when she was leaving to get married. 'Him sulky fella' they said about Dad's photograph, but what did they mean? There was action and excitement and fear, when she had handled a bolting four-in-hand and lived through an earthquake in Wyndham. It was living stuff and books could not compete with them (at least not the books available).

Mother had the ability to bring people alive when she talked about them. She did just that for Grandmother Kate (the dead one) when we asked about her and she told us that a visitor, calling on Grandmother Kate, found all the children roller-skating round and round the verandahs. 'How can you stand the noise,' she was asked, to which she promptly replied, 'Easily! When it is a happy noise.'

Mother told us that goat meat was despised by people even when they had never tasted it but that it was as good to eat as sheep meat—mutton it used to be called. There were no sheep on the Kimberley station when she kept house there, so whenever mutton was served, it was goat. If there were visitors, towards the end of the meal, one of the hosts would introduce the subject of goat meat and the typical visitor's comment would be 'You'd never get me eating goat!' So when the meal was over and visitors had expressed their appreciation of the delicious roast mutton, then and only then would they be told they had eaten goat.

And, as one memory stirs up another, I remember the country cousins telling us about the place the western train stopped for passengers to have a meal. When the waitress announced the menu of 'Mutton, goat or galah' and they ordered mutton, she further announced 'Mutton's off! Goat or galah.' Do you think they were pulling our legs?

Dad had plenty of good stories too, about his life at sea on a cable-laying ship and the wonderful, fantastic creatures that were dredged up from beneath the sea when the cable was being laid down; of volcanoes in the Hawaiian Islands and a shipwreck on Midway Island. Those were Dad's true stories but he also had some pretty hilarious fiction to tell when he was in the mood. Mother had told a true story about a policeman who was taken by a crocodile in Cambridge Gulf. Dad's fictional story of a policeman taken by a crocodile was quite different and we do not remember it coming to an end, so possibly it got too rough and Mother created a diversion to end it subtly. The image of a crocodile spitting out the brass buttons off the policeman's uniform remains vivid.

All children love to hear stories of their parents and grandparents as children, perhaps because they emphasize the human rather than the parental qualities in them. A story Dad told against himself amused us. When he was a boy he had been keen on acrobatics, gymnastics it may have been, and one day when he was practising in the front garden, a passer-by advised him that the way to loosen up the joints was to give them a good oiling and suggested a large dose of castor-oil. It worked but it didn't help the gymnastics.

Summer Holidays

Irish cousins

Whenever the Irish cousins came to town, which frequent droughts out in that dry land prevented from happening very often, they wanted to see as much as possible of their city cousins. It is strange how we remember them as Irish when they were second generation Australian, so they must have become irretrievably imbued with the nature of the stories of their really Irish uncles. The big day was a family get-together in the Botanic Gardens. Hold it! That couldn't be right. It must have been in the nearby Domain because of the presence of that slippery slide in the snapshots. Today's people wouldn't know about the Domain for it is no longer there. During the Second World War it was used for the erection of 'temporary' buildings and no one has found it since.

Someone somewhere has photographs to recall those picnics; in particular the ones on the slippery slide where the cousins are scaled up in age. There could never be any future doubt about who was older or younger than who, when that photograph was in a family album.

Those town and country mixings were not entirely the universal successes that the older generation planned them to be, for some town children cannot abide country people and the reverse applies also. That was not the only generation where this antipathy has been embarrassing to families.

Because all members of the family were fair-skinned, summer holidays were never at the beach. The country was favoured, in particular where we could benefit from some mountain air. Bundaberg was not exactly altitudinous but it was high in the number of Dad's friends. On a visit to one of these families, it was absolutely imperative, as only childish intuition can be, to see what was outside the kitchen window. In climbing on to a chair for the purpose of reaching the window-sill, the breadboard, presumably scrubbed and left there to dry, was knocked down and, horror of horrors, what was outside the kitchen window was plainly revealed—two halves of a wooden breadboard on the ground below. The guilt was persistent and heavy for the confession had to wait seventeen years and, after all that suffering, it came as a shock to learn that those people did not remember the broken breadboard at all.

There was a time we rented Wirra Wirra, lovely name to appeal to children and easy to remember over half a century. It was a charming old home on the range in Toowoomba with an orchard and a fowl-run behind it. The novelty of feeding the chooks was all absorbing. With the tender loving care those chooks were getting, the eggs increased until the eleven chooks were producing ten eggs daily. That meant one chook was not pulling its weight, so after very careful study, the culprit was discovered and a most important aspect of a child's education was cleared up—roosters, it was learnt, did not lay eggs. Life is full of mysteries. Blackberries were part of that holiday too.

Once Glen Aplin, three thousand feet up, was chosen. That holiday was memorable for three things. One, the stationmaster of the little railway station took us for rides on the railway trolley. Two, we searched and searched for diamonds but did not find any. Three, it was discovered that a ten-year-old child could eat so much trifle, she had to be put to bed or shame the family.

It was certainly on a train, and probably on the train journey to Glen Aplin, that we noticed a decided change in Mother's character. Come to think of it, maybe she was 'letting her hair down' at the thought of a holiday in a hotel when, for three blissful weeks she would not have to cook a meal, make a bed or sweep a floor. She was almost skittish. Now, it isn't often mothers forget for a time that they are

43

mothers and respectable citizens, responsible for bringing up children to be nicely behaved young ladies and gentlemen. Of course, it was not so uncommon with Dad, especially after a good win at the races. His reading aloud of Chic Sale's *The Specialist*, with actions, will never be forgotten.

Every train-traveller knows the instructions on the wall of a train lavatory (it would be too disillusioning to learn they are no longer there!) and the song that went with them which Mother taught us:

> Passengers will please refrain
> from passing water while the train
> is standing at the station for awhile.
> If he feels he really orta,
> he can call a railway porter...

But, sadly, the last line or two have escaped from memory and the only person found who admitted knowing any said they were a parody from war days and he could not say them.

The tradespeople

In the category of our friends were the tradespeople—two in particular. First there was that friendly man who delivered the groceries and brought a bag of boiled lollies for the children. The lollies were the treat but the bag was important, too, because it was not an ordinary paper bag but a rectangle of paper twisted into a cone-shaped container. Obviously it did not hold as many sweets as a square bottomed bag but it gave to the grocer's delivery man a fine distinction, an admirable status. He was clever, like those people who could fold serviettes in fancy shapes.

John Chinaman, the greengrocer, was a much-loved, generous man, too. He once gave his customer a beautiful blue and white bowl of ginger for Christmas, but he was remembered more for his happy, smiling, laughing face; perhaps his laugh might more truthfully be described as a giggle. His voice was funny too—everything about him was funny. There were some children who used to run behind his cart calling out cheeky things like

'Turn-e-up and let-us-ee'

but, of course, the children of respectable, God-fearing, good Christian-living families would never behave in such an unbecoming way—not them!

> Ching chong Chinaman, velly, velly sad.
> Me afraid all de trade, velly, velly bad.
> No joke, brokey broke, makee shutee shop,
> Ching chong Chinaman, chop, chop, chop.

It is here we need to remember a chore that particular generation was spared, which was marketing, because all the tradespeople called for orders and delivered those orders. It was only when something in the order had been forgotten that the children were sent on errands to the little corner shop down the road, for a pound of butter or a dozen eggs. The latter was a great responsibility when each egg was separately wrapped in newspaper and all placed together in a paper bag. There were often casualties with such a delicate assignment. The reward was a penny for an ice-cream or only a halfpenny which would purchase some 'gumboils' of the sugary sweet kind. A penny would also buy a Lamp-post, which was a pyramid-shaped confection on the end of a stick. These came in red, green and yellow and it would be interesting to know what the shopkeepers did with all the leftover reds and greens which no child with worldly knowledge of such important matters would buy, because the reds were made from Red Indians' blood and the green were deadly poisonous. Gospel!

Climbing trees

There are always people who are luckier than the average. People like those who had large spreading trees just made for climbing, and these trees usually grew just inside the front fence so that they spread their branches over the footpath. Children could hide up in those branches and watch the people walking along below. Some children, who could have been expected to behave in a manner suited to their parents' respectable, church-going status in the community, would actually spit on the pedestrians below—or try to, for timing and aiming one's spit isn't *that* easy.

There were Bunya Pines in the garden too. They were not for climbing; certainly not for white children although we knew the Aborigines climbed them for the cones, but none of them were around to climb our trees. They must have had hard skin on their hands and feet. We had to wait for the cones to fall and we roasted the nuts in the living-room fireplace. Dad liked his boiled in the corned-beef water, and as usual Mother saw to it that everyone's tastes were catered for.

Very old frangipanni trees could be climbed by little children but not by big ones—they were too heavy and could break off the branches.

The best trees to climb were Moreton Bay figs and camphor laurel. Camphor laurels were good providers of games for, apart from the climbing of them which was easy, the berries could be used in various ways like produce in make believe shops and for making scent, but when that scent was put on the face it left a stain that was hard to wash off.

Lobbies

Other lucky families had waterholes or creeks and in those pools were lobbies. Outside Queensland people called them yabbies, but in Queensland they are lobbies or, to be more specific, to the purists they are freshwater crayfish. It was tremendously exciting catching them and the commercially minded child could receive threepence each for them from fathers who were partial to such gourmet fare. They could probably have pushed the price up to sixpence for the larger ones but as it was, threepence looked like overcharging to children more used to the brown coins. From every angle it was a very popular sport, so it will now be described in detail for the benefit of those people who may never have known this wonderful way of life.

First, a kind mother had to supply meat bones which were well and truly picked over on the way to the creek. A piece of string was tied to the bone—not white string because the lobbies could see that and stay down in the mud. Next, the bone was lowered into the water and, if you were sitting on a rail of a fence over the water, the string would be tied around it. Paddock fences were always the post-and-rail sort in those days. According to some of the experts, it was absolutely necessary to keep quiet while other experts insisted that stones should first be thrown into the pool to wake up the lobbies. No statistics were kept. The fisher for lobbies (would he be called a lobbier or a lobbyist?) would sit quietly watching the string and if it jerked that meant a lobby was feeding on the meat, so very carefully and very steadily the bone was raised a few inches from the surface; how far depended on the clarity of the water and if a head and claws could be seen then a rusty billy or tin was lowered into the water a little distance away to the side; it had to be rusty to be the same colour as the water so the lobby wouldn't see it; and then it would be brought up under the bone with the lobby clinging to it—caught with the greatest skill. Sometimes there were two caught together which made it all the more exciting.

There was always a king lobby—an awe-inspiring large creature that was sometimes glimpsed but never, never caught. It had all the mystery and wonder of a bunyip or the Sandy Cape Monster.

There was magic in catching lobbies in the creek—*forbidden* magic, as kill-joys always regard simple enjoyment as suspect. What right have people to get pleasure out of the simple things that do not have to be paid for? It violates the law of economics, and, as everyone knows, when you have to pay for your pleasures then it follows that you must enjoy them more. So the Shire Council came and turned that magical creek with its waterholes and mysterious king lobby into a drain because they said it bred mosquitoes. There were just as many mosquitoes afterwards in a world that could never be the same again.

The Old House

The house had been built in the 1860s and bought in 1911. Some of the furniture was of that time, some bought later, while a few pieces, brought by Dad's family from the Old Country, were older than the house.

The pictures on the living room wall were probably about the same vintage as the house—indubitably Victorian. They were large framed engravings depicting events in history. Over the mantelpiece was a soldier about to go to war, helmet at the ready, who was nursing a baby with one arm and embracing his wife with the other. What war he was off to was not clear but it was all very sentimentally moving because there was a baby in this house when Dad went off to war.

Another showed the sole survivor of the British invasion of Afghanistan, or one of those brave but stupid escapades the British involved themselves in around the romantic North-West Frontier. The poor bloke was in a state of near collapse in the centre of this large picture, with a sort of *Beau Geste* white fort in the background. Tragically stirring stuff, that one was.

The third was a war scene, possibly the Crimea War, with men and horses having a harassing time and right in the centre was a soldier dismounted with sword in hand. In later years when we had outgrown them, that one acquired the title 'Where's my bloody horse?' There was yet another of men in kilts, hiding behind some rocks with dogs and we thought that had something to do with Bonnie Prince Charlie because Grandmother Kate was somehow related to Flora MacDonald. It was classical Victoriana. Maybe one of these days we will find them in a folk museum and be

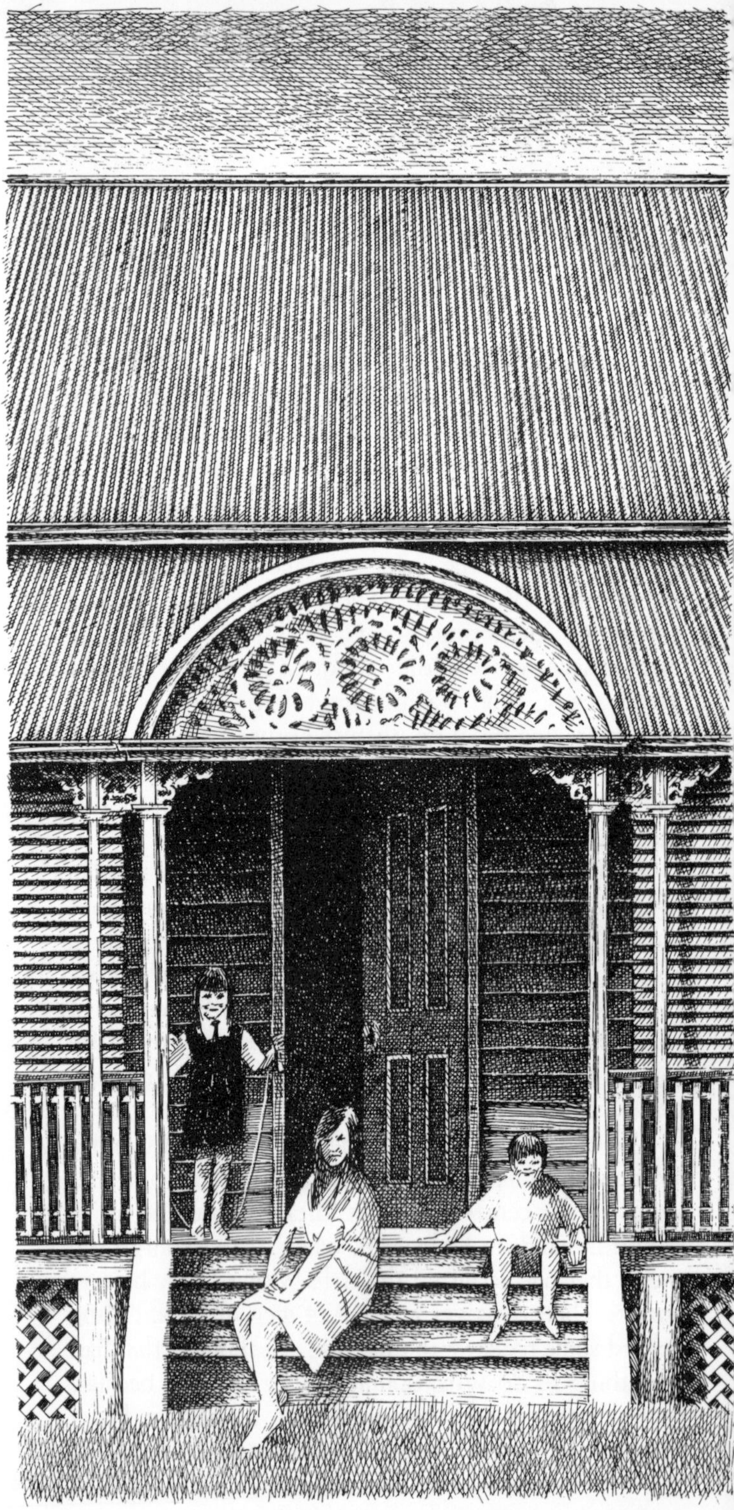

carried back into that room again. Look! The bookcase with the sliding glass doors beneath the poor chap on the North-West Frontier. Immediately it is slid open and a favourite book of all the family is extracted. It is a picture book although it was not meant for children. It is the collection of the Bainsfather cartoons of the First World War. We thought them very funny. There was that one of the two soldiers in the trench, with the caption 'If yer knows of a better 'ole, go to it.' Another was in two parts; the wife at home looking up to a full moon saying something about that same moon shining down on her beloved and the companion picture had the soldier in the trench cursing that very same moon for giving his position away.

Cardington was a most hospitable home. It was not thought to have been named after the pub of the same name, on the Houghton River, back o'Bowen in North Queensland where the colony's most colourful bushranger, James McPherson, 'The Wild Scotsman', first committed a crime, although coincidentally, this was also in the 1860s. In this warm, friendly house there always seemed to be people 'staying'; staying for long or short visits. One Western Australian cousin came for three weeks and stayed three months. How those parents put up with and even seemed to enjoy her stay, the young could not understand. In the lingo of the times she was considered to be 'as silly as a two-bob watch'.

Youthful visitors slept on the verandah in the row of stretchers, two by two between the French doors leading from the bedrooms. Each had a white quilt of the period and a mosquito net tied on to a tester at the head. This verandah had canvas blinds which were only strapped down when storms from the north drove rain on to the beds. This might happen in the middle of the night and anyone who slept through the noise and drama of getting the blinds untied, unrolled and strapped to the floor was accused of 'just pretending to be asleep' and too selfish to help, letting others do all the work.

Older visitors occupied the guest room and slept in the high double bed. Sometimes these polite people would allow their hosts' young to crawl in with them in the very early mornings. Both Cardington and its visitors were hospitable.

An uncle once came to stay who was into making garden gnomes. Being fifty years ahead of the fashion it was not a success and for years afterwards we stubbed our toes on concrete gnomes used as door stops. Just think what the suburban landscape was saved.

Vegetable garden

Cardington's vegetable garden was worked by Mr Wall. What do the sisters remember about the vegetable garden? One remembers always being sent to get a few 'sprigs of marjoram' for seasoning the stuffing of chooks. Another said, 'Nothing really, except that there were always vegetables in it, but I was very fond of Mr Wall.' The Ugly Duckling remembers eating lots of green peas and pulling up baby carrots by the score. It was no wonder she was fat.

They all remember the patch of sugar-cane, surprisingly as none of them were partial to chewing through the fibrous stalks, but the neighbourhood boys would appear on the back doorstep and say: 'Please, Missus, can I have a stick of sugar-cane?' and they remember that.

Mrs Wall

Mr Wall was the husband of Mrs Wall who did the washing. Mother had some favourite stories about Mrs Wall. It is only to be supposed that when two women wash side by side they would learn a great deal about each other. One story was that when Dad came back from the war he brought all odd socks with him which Mother gave to Mrs Wall for Mr Wall's work socks and she reported having found a mate for each of them. Mrs Wall thought Mr Wall was so handsome in his tan shoes when she married him.

Mother was not nearly so 'Victorian' as most women of her time but she was strongly of the opinion that pregnancy was undignified and she dieted strictly to keep her weight down and was always well corseted. By these means she hid her condition as long as possible. One day just when little sister was due to arrive, she complained to Mrs Wall of not feeling too well, to which that character replied: 'And to think I didn't know until last week that you were in trouble again.'

Haunted house

There was a road, a lonely road with only one big house in it, right in the bush past everyone else and children were strictly forbidden to go near it. Why? Because it was haunted. That provided food for some pretty heavy bragging.

'I know where there is a haunted house.'

'What is a haunted house?'

'It's a house that has a ghost in it and it's all scary and no one will live in it so it's always closed up with blinds drawn on the windows.'

'Really? What's this house like?'

Although having driven past it in a car only once, anything so interesting is indelibly photographed on to the memory.

'Oh, it looks just like lots of other houses. It has an upstairs and a downstairs and it's painted white. The only difference from other houses is a red light over the front door. Mother says a red light over the front door is to keep the mosquitoes away.'

I wish I was a fascinating bitch,
I'd never be poor and I'd always be rich.
I'd sleep all day and I'd work all night
In a little white house with a little red light.

Once a month I'd take a holiday
Just to make my customers wild.
Oh, I wish I was a fascinating bitch
And not an illegitimate child.

Green frogs

Children who have a sense of wonder, whether developed through encouragement or present by instinct, will find the world around them rich in entertainment; for instance those green frogs which, before the days of cane toads, could be found in cool places like letter boxes and around water meters and which felt funny when held in the hands. They were cold and soft—and so beautiful. Some children said they gave you warts and so they should not be picked up, but those children were not blessed with a sense of wonder, were they?

Daisy chains

Then there were the lovely necklaces which could be made from flowers. Daisy chains were one kind although they were not made from daisies at all, but from clover flowers that came through the lawn. It was so easy to make them, just a slit in the stalk of one made with the thumb nail and the stem of the next one is slipped through it. How the final two were linked, if they were, has been lost to memory. Perhaps they were just wound round and round the neck. The other kind we made by pushing a grass straw through the wind-fallen frangipanni flowers that covered the ground beneath the tree.

Underneath the house

When houses were on stumps there was space for children to play underneath the house in those parts too low for adults to put all those things that they never used but wouldn't throw away or couldn't because they were stored there for a bachelor uncle. That was where the little ferns grew, little ferns that could be dug up and planted in tins which then became secrets. Secrets were shared with very special friends, and gardens provided lots of material for secrets such as the buds of flowers that went pop when hit on the forehead, referred to as 'buddy fings' which made some people say 'What was *that* you said?' Then there were the daisies that told you who you would marry—tinker, tailor, soldier, sailor, rich man, poor man, beggarman, thief. And also when—this year, next year, sometime, never.

Possums, flying foxes and dingoes

Some children were so very deprived because they did not live in old houses, the houses possums liked best; possums that would come to the kitchen door and look so beautiful, which meant they wanted something to eat, a banana for preference but they would settle for a slice of bread in lieu. After being out all night they returned home at first light in the morning as noisy as drunks with their thumping across the iron roof. Deprived children who had no acquaintance with possums were frightened by the noise of possums coming home after a night out. They were also scared by the screeching noise made by the colony of flying foxes in the Moreton Bay fig tree near the house; or the wailing call of bush curlews or the howling of dingoes—all exciting sounds for children with imagination and the security of being tucked-up in their own beds with parents ready to be called upon, if necessary.

Brothers and Sisters

Little boys

Little girls had little brothers and those little brothers had little friends, all abominable children who did things no respectable, God-fearing, good Christian-living family would countenance, like putting tacks right across the road to cause punctures in all the friendly neighbours' car tyres. Putting pennies on the tramline was one thing that did not harm anything but the penny, but tacks across the road was vandalism that is supposed to be only part of our modern society with its social problems, and that was fifty years ago and more, and you could go back a further fifty years and still find such vandalism. People don't change. Little boys of every generation are naughty.

They are not just naughty. They are disgusting—smoking cow dung rolled in dirty newspaper—ugh!

They were an embarrassment, too. There is always a risk in taking irrepressible little boys to church even when disaster is guarded against and a child's prayer book with coloured illustrations is provided. It is quite impossible to foresee the directions of a child's mind especially when he is being angelically quiet, and then, in an enthusiastically loud voice, on seeing the picture of Zacchaeus in the tree, comes out with: 'Hey Mum! Look at Jesus up a tree after birds' nests.'

When young brother went to kindergarten he had his mouth washed out with soap and water for using bad words. It was some years later, the soap and water treatment not having been successful, when he dropped a 'bugger' in Dad's presence. Dad used a different method. 'Do you know what that word means?' No! 'Then go and look it up in the dictionary, and find out.' Bugger: one who commits buggery; a sodomite. 'What's a sodomite? Look it up!' Sodomite: one who practises or commits sodomy ... and so on. All that beating about the bush; really Mr Oxford needed pinning down, to get the lesson complete, although it is possible the end result may have brought confusion rather then enlightenment.

> What are little boys made of, made of?
> What are little boys made of?
>> Frogs and snails
>> And puppy-dogs tails,
> That's what little boys are made of.
>
> What are little girls made of, made of?
> What are little girls made of?
>> Sugar and spice
>> And all things nice,
> That's what little girls are made of.

Opera

This next story from our Bread and Dripping Days shows little girls as not always behaving nicely. Spice? Yes, some of that in their make-up, but sugar? Certainly not under such circumstances!

The best made plans of parents have a habit of going strangely awry because the children do not always understand what it is all about, so they could not possibly know how to respond. Some parents are culturally ambitious for their charges which is quite beyond the comprehension of the free and easy, wild or not totally restrained young. There were times when parents forgot they were children once, like when they took the kids to the opera and it was all sung in Italian. Well, that was good for a giggle. In fact, never again could they hear opera without wanting to send it up. After that they would turn on opera like turning on a tap, any day, anywhere, anyhow, with no need for an audience; the music was original, that is if it could be called music at all; the words at least were usually original. The production was modern with no need for settings or costumes.

It could also be used to great advantage, such as lightening the load of unpleasant, dreary chores, like the washing-up. Washing-up was always the scene of sisterly bickering, spitfire fights and generally nasty behaviour quite unbecoming in the best of families. But all that was B.O. (before opera). Opera provided an outlet for the emotions, getting rid of ill-feeling creatively. It worked like this: the scene is set in the kitchen, the characters are three sisters. It is the ugly sister's turn to wash up (she is not the same as the Ugly Duckling!). Hers is a small 'u' ugly. She does her turn of washing-up with bad grace and it is that bad grace which is always the cause of the lack of sisterly love in the vicinity of the kitchen sink. The ugly sister is the 'white-haired girl' of the parents, the father's 'little girl' and the mother's 'pride and joy'. To her sisters she is a pain in the neck, a bit of a sook, far too precious for them. The mirror on the wall did not show her as ugly, not at all. In fact, she was quite beautiful really, with fair curly hair and a rosebud mouth, clear fine skin (she wasn't an outdoor type), and she was *supposed* to be a little delicate, which was most convenient for her. Mentally she was as tough as Aboriginal string. The neighbours with babies loved her because she 'adored' babies and would spend all her spare time minding the local babies while her uncouth sisters played football or rounders with the rough boys in the street.

Back to the stage; the ugly sister doesn't like getting her hands dirty so she is too slow for her dryer-uppers who, inspired by the red in the tea-towels, begin a bull fight and that suggests the right words for a little bit of opera.

Tor-e-a-dor, don't spit on the floor,
Use the cuspidor, that's what its for...

At which stage, the ugly sister, with both hands pressed to her stomach, says, 'I've got to go.' Which in turn sets off:

She needs to go to the lavatory,
She needs to go to the lavatory,
She needs to go to the lavatory,
And so say all of us!

clasping their tummies too.

> She doesn't like washing the pots and pans,
> She doesn't like washing the pots and pans,
> She doesn't like washing the pots and pans
> And neither do the rest of us,
> And neither do the rest of us,
> And neither do the rest of us.
>
> We don't like washing the pots and pans,
> We don't like washing the pots and pans,
> We don't like washing the pots and pans
> so we will form a queue...

Nowadays sisters squabble over who will put the dishes in the washing-up machine, so you see, children from one generation to another don't change.

Parents are always keen for their children to learn to play a musical instrument and Mother was particularly so because she was not a bit musical. She said it was the result of hating her piano teacher who had hit her on the fingers with a ruler when she played a wrong note. Unfortunately, although her children had more kindly music teachers, it became obvious that an ear for music was simply not there in the genes they had inherited. This misfortune was plainly demonstrated when one of them, to escape from piano lessons, expressed a desire for violin lessons. If there had been only one person in the establishment with an 'ear' it would have been agony for him, but there wasn't one, not until the time of little sister, by which time the others had given up. At least she managed to sing in tune, or so we were told, for we couldn't tell. That was why our opera was so excrutiatingly funny.

It is not long since little sister recalled when brother began school she used to walk to the front gate with him each morning and kiss him goodbye. One day, possibly after a 'tiff' between them, she very nearly didn't but relented at the last moment and ran up to him just in time. He was pleased, of course, but warned her, 'You nearly missed out this time.' It all came back to her when he paid her a visit and she nearly missed out again by being delayed and had to race up to him just as he was boarding the coach, to give him her sisterly kiss. She said he still smiled as he did as a five-year-old.

At the Dinner Table

To think of the family of the twenties is to see all at the dining table in the social hour of the day. Father is at the head, mother on his right and the eldest on his left, descending by age down the sides, so the youngest was forever asking for something to be 'passed'.

Table mats hadn't come in. There were tablecloths, white tablecloths whether cotton or linen; starched tablecloths they were and starched serviettes in the member's own serviette ring which usually was a christening present from a godparent and engraved with the name and date of birth.

Dad did the carving, first sharpening the carving knife on a steel. Mother served the vegetables and later the puddings, and no one commenced eating until all were served. That, said Mother, was only good manners but it was also plain commonsense, for otherwise the first served would be back for 'seconds' before the last served had a chance to begin eating.

There was a time when the table was set with the dessert spoon and fork above, the fork facing left and the spoon to the right. The time came when eldest sister said this was old-fashioned and they should be set inside the knife and fork on the sides. She also objected, for the same reason, to the fork being placed upside down beside the knife, when the serving was finished. While such a wise mother would not have been concerned about being thought old-fashioned by a slip of a girl, it was always more peaceful to placate that strong-minded girl, at least in matters of no consequence. It would have been about the same time that puddings became sweets.

Straight backs were insisted on and when Mother said, 'Boy, sit up straight,' all shoulders went back, including Dad's. No elbows on the table either. It was not really so strict as it was manageable and it did provide a good setting for conversation which was usually animated. Many and varied were the subjects discussed and, if there was a difference of opinion, Dad ordered 'Look it up right now.' We did and if he came off second best then, of course, the dictionary or encyclopedia was wrong.

It was quite different at breakfast when Dad read the paper and the children were able to come and go in their own time or even learn their spellings for the day's lessons. It was not necessary to ask to be excused from the breakfast table either.

Some table manners were considered silly but were learnt nevertheless. Butter knives were tiresome little tools but the butter dish was not to be messed up with crumbs and jam. Why were we made to break our bread but allowed to cut the toast? No reason given. And why did the pepper and salt have to be put on the edge of the plate and not shaken over the meal? People had such funny ideas about what was right and what was wrong. There were still some people around who left a little food on their plate 'for good manners'. We thought that was senseless but the funniest good manners of all were ladies who crooked their little finger when holding a teacup. We called that 'la de da'. And when we played ladies' tea-parties we always did it, and our speech also, on such occasions was exaggeratedly 'la de da'.

The most absurd rule of all was eating peas from the back of the fork. Unless they could be embedded in mashed potato, they went rolling down the slope, as likely as not scattering over the spotless tablecloth. By way of contrast, the next generation of children were allowed to carry their peas in the bowl of the fork, accompanied by this little bit of irreverence:

> I eat my peas with honey.
> I've done it all my life.
> It may seem rather funny,
> but it keeps them on the knife.

The End of an Era

The era recognized as Bread and Dripping Days really ended when the 1860s rear part of the house was brought into the second decade of the 20th century. The 'period' facade was not changed but much of the internal life style was. Of course, this could well have had something to do with the children shaping up with the promise of growing up.

While the changes made were much more suitable for a growing up family and more comfortable, we lost so much of the dear, old and familiar, like the back verandah and the walk-in pantry. It is a funny thing about that pantry, for looking into it now, all those shelves are empty; there is nothing there but the bottle of horse emollient. It stands out so clearly one can almost read the label 'relief of stiff muscles'. If it would work on a horse then it should also work when a child had aching muscles. The result, like the contents of the shelves, has faded right away, but it could not have been of no consequence to have survived for half a century.

And the lumber room of many happy days went, too. If a sociologist had designed the perfect playroom for children on wet days, then that lumber room was the model. It was full of articles that stimulated the imagination, challenged the initiative, stirred the creative instincts. It was a room full to the brim of unemployed things, waiting for rehabilitation to be put back into use. So what became of all those things? A mother who believed in 'waste not, want not', even to the extent of making soap when she had an accumulation of dripping, would have had to find homes for all those things. What a job! Perhaps they too went to 'the creche'.

A day in the life of a child is an eternity. To live every moment of it is tiring, so, when the day is at its end, all good children need to go to bed early so they may wake fresh to meet with full zest what is ahead. Kiss Dad goodnight. 'Clean your teeth and say your prayers.' Into nighties and jump into the beds lined up along the verandah. Now the lovely Mother does her rounds, tucking-up and giving her goodnight kisses. 'Did you remember to say your prayers? No? Well, never mind getting out of bed again, we'll all say one together; you repeat each line after me:

> Here I lay me down to sleep
> and pray to God my soul to keep;
> and if I die before I wake,
> I pray to God my soul to take.
>
> There are four corners on my bed,
> there are four angels at my head.
> Matthew, Mark, Luke and John,
> bless the bed that I lie on.'